How Great Is Your Guy?

How Great Is Your Guy?

SARAH CHRISTENSEN FU

ILLUSTRATIONS BY
KATIE ABEY

This book is dedicated to
my wonderful husband, Andrew Fu.

Contents

Introduction

Archaeologists say that sometime around 35,000 years ago the first Homo sapiens evolved from Neanderthals. These early humans were hunters and gatherers, lived in small groups, and cooked their meat outdoors over a fire. Courtship during this era is thought by some to have involved the male of the species hefting his chosen mate— most likely the one with the widest childbearing hips—over his shoulder in order to stir up some Paleolithic-style cave romance.

While courtship rituals have certainly evolved since the Paleolithic era, it's clear that even today physical strength and sharp mental attributes are still desirable factors, and can aid in attracting a worthy and suitable mate.

To pass muster in days past, a man basically had to run fast enough to hunt, be clever enough to find water, and strong enough to impress his mate. Today's man has a much wider proving ground.

A suitable modern male must be a master of the remote control, a connoisseur of craft beer, and, of course, he must also remember his partner's birthday. He must be a student of pop culture, literature, and music, and be knowledgeable in mathematics—at least enough to tip properly and pay his annual taxes. Yes, the modern man must smell good, while still getting his hands dirty. He must remember his partner's favorite reality TV star and parallel park like a boss. He must know when to be strong and when to be sensitive, and to never confuse the two. Or at least try, anyway.

But how can potential mates know what skills a man actually has, and what he is lacking? How can these skills be quantified and compared in order to create a snapshot of his viability as a long-term partner?

This book contains a series of tests designed for you to get to know your man's ins and outs, and to help you gather enough data across key categories to make your final decision: Is your man a keeper, or should you toss him back? Remember, there are plenty of fish in the sea, so get ready, get set, and test your man.

Chapter One

Hygiene Habits

He could be tall, dark, and handsome. He could be rich. But if he's stinky and leaves a horrid yellow ring around the toilet, all bets are off. From leaving specks of toothpaste all over the bathroom mirror to eating food off the ground, different men have different levels of disgusting behavior. Measure your man to see if you are compatible with his hygiene habits.

1 Pheromones

It's science: In order to form a happy, sexy, quality relationship with your partner, your inner cavewoman must be attracted to the pheromones that he unwittingly sends out into the world. You experience his pheromones primarily through your sense of smell. Which of these is the closest to your reaction to finding a sweaty shirt that he left on the floor?

Wouldn't touch it with a ten-foot pole. **NIL POINTS**

You'd pick it up with a pair of tongs and rubber kitchen gloves and throw it immediately in a pot of boiling water or a very, very hot washing machine. **1 POINT**

It's a little annoying that it's on the floor (slob), but it doesn't stink. **2 POINTS**

You might give it a little loving sniff before throwing it in the hamper. **3POINTS**

You keep it hidden away under your pillow or in your desk drawer and bury your face in it regularly. **4 POINTS**

Total Score _____ (0–4 pts)

2 Bathroom Battleground

When you're dating, seeing your man's "personal" side can seem romantic and sweet. When you're living together and sharing a bathroom, however, it can be quite another story. How does your man score with his bathroom habits?

He has never heard of flushing, apparently. **NIL POINTS**

He flushes, but has useless little alligator arms when it comes to any sort of cleaning up. **1 POINT**

He keeps things sort of tidy, but his version of tidy is very, very different from yours. **2 POINTS**

He's actually too clean, making you extremely self-conscious about your own bathroom habits. **3 POINTS**

He splits the housework with you, and even wipes up those little hairs after he shaves. **4 POINTS**

Total Score _____ (0–4 pts)

3 Regular Maintenance

Good hygiene isn't a one-and-done sort of deal. It takes years, even decades, to establish great health and acceptable hygiene. Give your guy 1 point for each of the following good habits he practices.

He flosses every day. ☐

He visits the doctor regularly for physical check-ups. ☐

He shaves regularly. ☐

He wears clean socks every day. ☐

He applies deodorant on a daily basis. ☐

He showers every day. ☐

He gets his hair cut at least a few times a year. ☐

His breath is usually tolerable. ☐

He washes his hands after using the restroom. ☐

He minimizes burps, passing gas, and other sorts of bodily functions in public. ☐

Total Score _____ (0–10 pts)

4 Activity: Pop Quiz

You're the health inspector, and your man is under investigation. Can he pass the smell test or will his hygiene habits gross you out when you take a close look? Score him up to 2 points for each of the following:

	CLEANLINESS	SCENT
Hair		
Nails		
Breath		
Clothes		
Feet		
Armpits		
Private parts		
Total Score (0–28 pts)		

CHAPTER ONE: SCORING

Add up your score on each question to get your total score for Chapter One, then find out how your man measures up below.

Q1 Score _____ (0–4 pts)

Q2 Score _____ (0–4 pts)

Q3 Score _____ (0–10 pts)

Q4 Score _____ (0–28 pts)

Total Chapter Score _____ (0–46 pts)

34–46 pts: Your guy sparkles, at least in your eyes! He keeps it clean in every aspect of his life and doesn't have too many habits that disturb you.

21–33 pts: Your guy likes to keep tidy, but also lets himself relax and enjoys getting his hands dirty once in a while. Frankly, you probably don't mind too much when he does!

11–20 pts: So he's not the cleanest guy on the block. He's yours! You can suffer through the bad breath and even some body odor in order to get close to him, and he will make it up to you in other ways.

0–10 pts: Hygiene may be an area of contention in your relationship. Remember, you probably can't change your man's habits, so you may want to invest in nose plugs, potpourri, and a maid service to come in from time to time.

Chapter Two

Memory Mania

Once you meet and charm the man of your dreams, it would be nice if he could remember it. How well does your man's memory work when it comes to the important stuff?

1 Commemoration Recollection

Ask your partner to recall the following big dates.
Score 1 point for each date he can remember. Feel free to
substitute dates that may hold more importance to him
than the ones listed below.

The anniversary of the first time you met. ☐

The anniversary of the first time you said "I love you." ☐

Your birthday. ☐

Your pet's birthday. ☐

Your best friend's birthday. ☐

Your mother's birthday. ☐

His parents' wedding anniversary. ☐

Your parents' wedding anniversary. ☐

Total Score _____ (0–8 pts)

2 Fact vs. Fiction

Can your man determine the difference between things that have happened to you and the plot of popular coming-of-age movies? Take a few moments to fill in the blanks with details about the plot of your life, and then see if he can guess which events are fact and which are fiction. Award him 1 point for each answer he gets correct.

That time when my parents wouldn't let me play soccer, but I lied to them and snuck away, and we won the championship and they ended up being really proud of me.

(Movie: *Bend It Like Beckham*) ☐

That time when I _____

_____ ☐

That time when I walked for two days with my friends to go see a dead body.

(Movie: *Stand by Me*) ☐

That time when I _____

_____ ☐

That time when I moved to a new school and I infiltrated the popular girls by posing as their friend, and got caught up in it all.

(Movie: *Mean Girls*) ☐

That time when I _____

_____ ☐

Total Score _____ (0–6 pts)

3 School Daze

Matching! What does your guy remember from his days as a schoolboy? Can he connect the topics on the left with the lessons on the right? Give him 1 point for each one he can match correctly.

1. The Theory of Relativity   **a.** Philosophy

2. Existentialism   **b.** Mathematics

3. Chaos Theory   **c.** Physics

4. Iambic Pentameter   **d.** Literature

Total Score _____ (0–4 pts)

4 Activity: Grocery Guerilla

Oh no, you need your man to stop by the store on the way home, and your phone is running out of batteries—he must remember it all! Recite the following list to him and then set a timer for 15 minutes to see if he can recall all the items. Score 1 point for each item he can remember, and an extra point if he can remember the quantity of each item.

	ITEM (0–1 PT)	QUANTITY (0–1 PT)
8 apples		
18 apricots		
3 yellow plums		
2 yellow peppers		
3 banana peppers		
9 ripe bananas		
1 bar of 72% dark chocolate		
Total Score (0–14 pts)		

CHAPTER TWO: SCORING

Add up your score on each question to get your total score for Chapter Two, then find out how your man measures up below.

Q1 Score _____ (0–8 pts)

Q2 Score _____ (0–6 pts)

Q3 Score _____ (0–4 pts)

Q4 Score _____ (0–14 pts)

Total Chapter Score ____ (0–32 pts)

26–32 pts: Your man's mind is a steel trap! This is excellent news when you want him to remember an important event, but less great when he brings up that one time you were wrong.

17–25 pts: "Remember that time, right after we first met, when you were wearing that red top and I was eating a hot dog?" Your man remembers certain things, and has completely blocked out others. Hopefully, he remembers the right things!

8–16 pts: It's not that he's not a bright boy, it's just that his memory isn't his strong suit. Your man can solve complex problems, but he will likely never remember the name of the perfume you wear, or the date you first flirted, or the cocktail you were sipping at the time.

0–7 pts: Life with this man will be a little bit like life with a person who is suffering from amnesia. Just focus on the present moment and enjoy one another's company, and if it's very important for him to remember something, leave him a note in his lunchbox.

Chapter Three

On the Menu

Some say the quickest way to a woman's heart is through her stomach. Others say it's by complimenting her barely there, extra-flat abdominals. Either way, a man who knows what's on the menu is vital to a woman's health and happiness. Does your man know how to delight your tastebuds?

1 Bartender

Make it a double! Award the number of points that most closely aligns with your partner's bartending ability. Whether it's coffee, tea, wine, beer, or a cocktail, can your man make your favorite drink?

He keeps getting your favorite drinks mixed up with his ex's and/or his mother's. **NIL POINTS**

He is pretty sure that his favorite drink is your favorite drink, and won't hear otherwise. **1 POINT**

He can name your favorite drink, he'll order it for you at a restaurant, and if someone else buys all the ingredients, he could probably make it. **2 POINTS**

He never lets your favorite drink—or the ingredients to make it—run too low before making a run to the nearest store. **3 POINTS**

He's got your favorite drink waiting for you before you even ask. **4 POINTS**

Total Score _____ (0–4 pts)

2 Figure Factors

It's not easy to keep your youthful figure. Can your man keep track of which diets you have tried in order to stay healthy and fit? Award him 1 point for each diet that you've tried that he correctly identifies.

No- or low-carbohydrate diet. ☐

Cutting wheat or gluten. ☐

Cutting dairy, such as cheese and cream. ☐

Cutting sugar. ☐

Cutting alcohol and/or soda. ☐

See-food diet (when you see food, you eat it). ☐

No- or low-calorie diet. ☐

Paleolithic or caveman diet. ☐

Vegetarian or fruitarian diet. ☐

Detox or cleansing diet. ☐

Total Score _____ (0–10 pts)

3 Comfort Food

Forget the diet! When you need comfort and just want
to dig in to your favorite meal, does your man know
how to make it happen? Award him 1 point for each of
your beloved comfort foods that he correctly identifies.
Feel free to substitute those listed with your own favorites.

Pizza. ☐   Ice cream. ☐

Chocolate. ☐   Kale chips. ☐

Mac and cheese. ☐   Spicy food. ☐

Salad greens. ☐   Bacon. ☐

Fried chicken. ☐   Popcorn, crisps, or pretzels. ☐

Total Score ____ (0–10 pts)

4 Activity: Soup to Nuts

Cook up a storm! Can your partner plan and prepare a meal that you love, from soup to nuts? Rate him on the flavor, presentation—and don't forget to award extra points for a positive attitude while cooking!

	FLAVOR (0–6 PTS)	PRESENTATION (0–6 PTS)	ATTITUDE (0–6 PTS)
Appetizer			
Main Course			
Dessert			
Total Score (0–18 pts)			

CHAPTER THREE: SCORING

Add up your score on each question to get your total score for Chapter Three, then find out how your man measures up below.

Q1 Score _____ (0–4 pts)

Q2 Score _____ (0–10 pts)

Q3 Score _____ (0–10 pts)

Q4 Score _____ (0–18 pts)

Total Chapter Score _____ (0–42 pts)

30–42 pts: Not only does your man have an excellent sense of your favorite foods and drinks, he also doesn't mind getting his hands dirty in the kitchen. Food is love, and he loves you … a lot!

20–29 pts: Your man enjoys good food and is glad that you enjoy it with him.

10–19 pts: You and your man won't starve, but you might be missing out on some awesome bonding over delicious foods. Try branching out and trying new things!

0–9 pts: Some people live to eat, some eat to live. It seems like food isn't the top priority on your relationship's agenda.

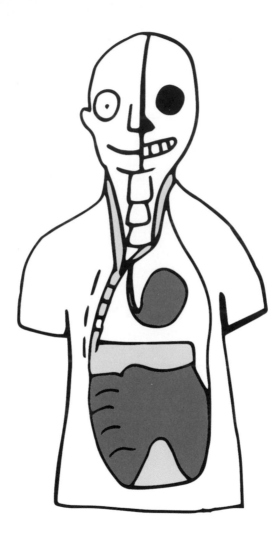

Chapter Four

Anatomy Action

Past head, shoulders, knees, and toes, does your man have an intricate knowledge of the human body and how to work it? Set him the anatomy tests in this chapter and make him prove how well he knows all the ins and outs of the way your body works.

1 Which of These Parts Do You Have?

Some of the body parts below are real and some are invented. Read the list to your man and see which body parts he correctly identifies. Give him 1 point for each body part he gets right (answers in bold).

a) Real/Invented: Auriculares (ear wiggling muscles)

b) Real/**Invented**: Theocraniatic Muscle

c) Real/Invented: Coccyx (tailbone)

d) Real/**Invented**: Climphallacial Region

e) Real/Invented: Arrector Pili (goosebumps)

f) Real/**Invented**: Adennorthropex

Total Score _____ (0–6 pts)

2 Erogenous Zones

If there's one thing a man should know it's his partner's erogenous zones—you know, the parts of her body that drive her wild with desire when poked and prodded. Women have erogenous zones all over their body: from their feet to their ears. Choose the answer from the following that best describes your partner's mastery of your most sensitive areas.

He thinks your biggest erogenous zones are on his body.

NIL POINTS

Whenever he wants to activate your erogenous zones, he just turns on a sexy episode of *Mad Men* or *Game of Thrones*.

I POINT

You feel obliged to remind him what you like each time— and especially what you don't. (You may have muttered phrases like, "Please get your finger out of my ear.")

2 POINTS

After practically— or actually!—drawing him a map, he now successfully navigates the most sensitive parts of your body.

3 POINTS

He knows you better than you know yourself and can find all your erogenous zones, from the standard neck to that special spot on your left cheek. **4 POINTS**

Total Score _____ (0–4 pts)

3 'Till the End

The sad truth is that, statistically, men usually die earlier than women. How is your man taking care of his body in order to live long and prosper? Give him 1 point for each activity you've seen him do over the past few weeks.

Cardio workouts such as running or biking. ☐

Strength training. ☐

Meditation or prayer. ☐

Sleeping 8 hours plus per night. ☐

Playing outside, enjoying nature. ☐

Eating meals with healthy protein. ☐

Eating lots of greens and salads. ☐

Avoiding smoking and drugs. ☐

Total Score _____ (0–8 pts)

4 Activity: Drawn Together

Since the dawn of time, artists have studied the human anatomy to celebrate its beauty and functionality. In olden days, having a fine artist sketch you or paint your portrait was a huge honor. Can your man capture your very essence on the page in three poses? You can either pose for him or have him draw you from memory.

ROUND	1	2	3
Technique (0–2 pts)			
Feeling (0–2 pts)			
Effort (0–2 pts)			
Total Score, Round 1 (0–6 pts)			
Total Score, Round 2 (0–6 pts)			
Total Score, Round 3 (0–6 pts)			
Total Score (0–18 pts)			

CHAPTER FOUR: SCORING

Add up your score on each question to get your total score for Chapter Four, then find out how your man measures up below.

Q1 Score _____ (0–6 pts)

Q2 Score _____ (0–4 pts)

Q3 Score _____ (0–8 pts)

Q4 Score _____ (0–18 pts)

Total Chapter Score _____ (0–36 pts)

27–36 pts: Your man is master of his domain—and of yours. Enjoy his expert knowledge of the human body as regularly as possible!

19–26 pts: Your man has a healthy understanding of how to keep his body strong and his partner smiling.

10–18 pts: See if you can get your partner to turn up his anatomy game! Maybe a sweaty jog together, followed by a shower, could help pique his interest.

0–9 pts: So what if he gets confused when he sings "Head, shoulders, knees, and toes …"? Your guy is probably amazing with the remote control, and excellent at ordering takeout, which are very important skills.

Chapter Five

High Style

Some people have a flair for fashion and some just flop when it comes to keeping up with the latest styles. Is your man in the know or a fashion nincompoop?

1 Fashion Forward

Even if your partner is not the most fashionable person on the planet, it's helpful if he knows the basic vocabulary in order to hold a civilized conversation. Quiz your man: Read the words on the left and see if he can match each one to the type of clothing on the right. Award 1 point for each correct answer.

1. Espadrilles   **a.** Purse

2. Hobo   **b.** Dress

3. Sheath   **c.** Shoes

4. Gaucho   **d.** Tie

5. Cravat   **e.** Pants

Total Score _____ (0–5 pts)

Answers: 1c, 2a, 3b, 4e, 5d

2 How Do I Look?

Some men are great communicators. Some—not so much. Nowhere is awkward communication more apparent than when a partner asks that one ageless question while getting ready: "How do I look?" Choose the answer below that most closely resembles how your own man answers this question.

Just makes a face. **NIL POINTS**

Answers "fine" while not looking. **1 POINT**

"Well, the top is nice but the bottom makes you look kind of … er …" **2 POINTS**

"You look beautiful in anything you wear" **3 POINTS**

"I love it when you wear clothes that bring out your eyes. You've got great taste." **4 POINTS**

Total Score _____ (0–4 pts)

3 Man Style

Just because a man likes to look good doesn't make him prissy. Award your man 1 point for each occasion for which you think he would be able to put together an outfit—all on his own—which you deem appropriate and acceptable.

Black tie party. ☐

Family wedding. ☐

Football game. ☐

Neighborhood party. ☐

Job interview. ☐

Great aunt's funeral. ☐

School recital. ☐

Work conference. ☐

Favorite rock band concert. ☐

Date night. ☐

Total Score _____ (0–10 pts)

4 Activity: OMG, Shoes!

Does your partner have any idea what's lurking in your closet? Can he come close to estimating the pairs of thongs, sharp stilettos, criss-cross laces, and chunky heels that reside in your household?

Step 1) Ask him! Get him to estimate the total number of shoes you own as they fall into each category below.

	BLACK	BROWN	OTHER COLORS	METALLIC
Boots				
Heels				
Sneakers				
Sandals				
Other				

Step 2) Take an inventory. Write in the grid how many of each type of shoe you actually own.

	BLACK	BROWN	OTHER COLORS	METALLIC
Boots				
Heels				
Sneakers				
Sandals				
Other				

Step 3) Compare your answers. Give him 1 point for each shoe category he nailed (or, if you're feeling charitable, give him a point if he came close).

Total Score _____ (0–20 pts)

CHAPTER FIVE: SCORING

Add up your score on each question to get your total score for Chapter Five, then find out how your man measures up below.

Q1 Score _____ (0–5 pts)

Q2 Score _____ (0–4 pts)

Q3 Score _____ (0–10 pts)

Q4 Score _____ (0–20 pts)

Total Chapter Score _____ (0–39 pts)

30–39 pts: He knows what he's wearing and he's not scared to flaunt it. Not only that, he loves to see you look your best and lets you know how much he appreciates your sense of style! You compliment one another and look great together.

20–29 pts: This man will not embarrass you in public. He cleans up nicely. He's got enough fashion and flair to draw some attention, but not nearly enough to take the limelight away from you!

10–19 pts: Your man may need some guidance in the fashion department. Teach him, and make sure to reward his good efforts with a shopping trip.

0–9 pts: Warning: Your man may wear socks with sandals, brown belt with black shoes, and an extra-wide polka-dot tie. It's probably best to start finding his fashion blunders endearing.

Chapter Six

Ro-MAN-tic

Couples who have been together for decades give some very specific and very consistent advice for staying together in the long run. Laugh often, don't go to bed mad, and, above all else, keep the romance alive. Test your man to see if he has what it takes in the romance department to help your relationship go the distance.

1 Date Night

One way to keep romance alive is to make a regular date night. Then, no matter what else happens during the week, you and your partner won't miss the opportunity to go out together and paint the town red. What does date night look like in your household?

He watches TV while you clean the house, put the kids or pets to bed, and make dinner. Then he eats said dinner while watching TV. **NIL POINTS**

You haven't been able to schedule a date night in too long to remember, but the idea of one makes you both smile.
1 POINT

You always go to the same place and do the same thing—and it's getting old. **2 POINTS**

You sometimes go to the same place and do the same thing—but you both love it and it sparks romance.
3 POINTS

Always new and exciting, you and your man love planning epic date nights that leave you both feeling totally excited.
4 POINTS

Total Score _____ (0–4 pts)

2 A Rose Is But A Rose

For many women, small gestures can keep the romance alive, and flowers make a wonderful and sensual gift. But if your guy thinks that just any flower will do, he might be in for a sad surprise. Can he match the flowers in the left-hand column with their traditional meaning on the right? Award him 1 point for each correct answer.

1. Striped	a. Shyness
2. Yellow	b. Refusal, breakup
3. Sweetpea	c. Forgiveness
4. White	d. Desire for riches
5. Marigold	e. Friendship only

Total Score _____ (0–5 pts)

3 Ridiculously Romantic

Love is a universal language, but does your man speak it? Ask him to summarize the plot of these ridiculously romantic movies, and award him 1 point for each plot he gets close to (it's up to you to award him the point for creative interpretation).

Titanic
Actual: A poor boy and a wealthy girl fall in love, only to be separated forever when the ship sinks.

His: _____

Romeo and Juliet
Actual: Teen lovers separated by their families commit suicide.

His: _____

Doctor Zhivago
Actual: A rich businessman embraces the revolution until the woman he loves is exiled.

His: _____

Bridget Jones's Diary

Actual: A woman realizes she's in love with someone who's frustrated her in the past.

His: _____

The Fault in Our Stars

Actual: Two terminally ill teens fall in love.

His: _____

Jane Eyre

Actual: A governess and her employer fall in love and come together through tragedy.

His: _____

Total Score _____ (0–6 pts)

4 Activity: Chivalry Isn't Dead

Nothing makes a partner feel cherished and treasured like small displays of chivalry—other than large displays of chivalry, of course. When you and your man go out, does he treat you with courtly manners? Keep tabs on your next date night, and award him up to 2 points for each act of chivalry.

ATTEMPT	SCORE (0–2 PTS)
Offers a small gift.	
Opens doors.	
Shares umbrella or jacket. (If it's not raining or chilly, give him points if he's ever done this in the past.)	
Takes off hat or acknowledges when you enter a room.	
Treats you with respect and interest.	
Total Score (0–10 pts)	

CHAPTER SIX: SCORING

Add up your score on each question to get your total score for Chapter Six, then find out how your man measures up below.

Q1 Score _____ (0–4 pts)

Q2 Score _____ (0–5 pts)

Q3 Score _____ (0–6 pts)

Q4 Score _____ (0–10 pts)

Total Chapter Score _____ (0–25 pts)

19–25 pts: His heart beats for you, that much is true. You've got yourself a true romantic. Your man knows how to bring it, from gifts to kind gestures.

12–18 pts: Your man has romance running deep within his veins. Wake it up with a little romantic gesture of your own, and see where the evening takes you!

6–11 pts: It's hard to keep the romance alive during busy day-to-day life. Keep trying to initiate acts of love and you may find that your partner's romance score improves.

0–5 pts: Your guy doesn't see much of a need to be romantic with you. This is actually not so bad—it means he sees you as a true equal and treats you like a best friend. If you want to increase the romantic vibes in your relationship, try reminding him that you are a best friend—with benefits!

Chapter Seven

Handyman

A man who knows his way around a tool box is worth his weight in gold. Does your man know what to do in an emergency and how to help out around the house when push comes to shove?

1 Training and Preparation

Good men aren't born; they're trained. It will make your job much easier if your partner has undergone any of these training programs. Give your man 1 point for each one he's tried.

Boy Scouts. ☐

Little League sports. ☐

Marathon run or long race. ☐

Military training. ☐

Volunteer service. ☐

Peace Corps. ☐

Other. ☐

Total Score _____ (0–7 pts)

2 Survival Skills

Whether your man is very handy or can't change a lightbulb, you'll still rely on him to lend a hand if you face a natural disaster. Does your man have survival skills? Read him the following scenarios and ask him what he would do. Award him between 0–2 points, depending on how close he comes to answering correctly.

PROBLEM	SOLUTION
You're at home and a pipe bursts. Water begins to fill your home.	Find the water shut-off valve and start bailing out water. Call your insurance company as soon as possible.
The pilot in your private plane dies while you're in midair.	Look for a grove of trees to land in. They will absorb the shock. Avoid water and large open spaces.
You're behind the wheel of a car on a windy mountain road when your brakes stop working.	Ease into the guardrail to slow the car down. Ride along the guardrail until your car comes to a stop.
You've lost your way in the woods, and your cell phone has no service—once in a while it gets one bar for a brief moment—how do you get help?	Text all your friends and tell them where you are. Ask them to call 911 to help you.
You are out walking in your neighborhood and a dog starts chasing you.	Stay calm, don't run or make eye contact, squirt him with a water bottle if possible.
Total Score (0–10 pts)	

3 A Little Help?

When the "Honey-Do" list piles up and the work around the house starts to accumulate, can you count on your partner to help out? Which of these sounds most like the response you get when you ask for help with chores?

"Not a chance. I think that's your job." **NIL POINTS**

"Oh no, the old knee is acting up again. Better lie on the couch and watch TV." **I POINT**

"I'll do it next weekend." **2 POINTS**

"No problem, honey. As soon as the game's over."
3 POINTS

"I already did it! And everything else on the list. What else can I do?" **4 POINTS**

Total Score _____ (0–4 pts)

4 Activity: Zombie Apocalypse

It's not a matter of if—it's a matter of when. When the zombie apocalypse occurs, it's recommended to have a grab-and-go bag packed. What kind of things would your man pack in his bag? Ask him to name one item in each category and award him 1 or 2 points for everything he suggests that you think is essential to your family's comfort and survival.

	ITEMS (0–2 PTS)	PRACTICALITY (0–2 PTS)
Food and drink		
Communication		
Clothing		
Entertainment		
Protection		
First aid		
Total Score (0–24 pts)		

CHAPTER SEVEN: SCORING

Add up your score on each question to get your total score for Chapter Seven, then find out how your man measures up below.

Q1 Score _____ (0–7 pts)

Q2 Score _____ (0–10 pts)

Q3 Score _____ (0 4 pts)

Q4 Score _____ (0–24 pts)

Total Chapter Score _____ (0–45 pts)

35–45 pts: Whoa! The entire neighborhood is coming to your house in case of an emergency. Your man has an excellent grasp of what is needed when things go wrong. Also, if anyone needs a lightbulb changed, their lawn mowed, or their garbage taken out, your man might get a call.

24–34 pts: Good news, you can rest comfortably knowing that you will be safe if the unexpected goes down. Your man has a plan and isn't afraid to use it.

13–23 pts: You might want to start educating yourself in all the things that you need to do to maintain the house and protect yourself—and your partner—in an emergency.

0–12 pts: Not everyone can be handy or survive a natural disaster.

Chapter Eight

Compatibility

Some say opposites attract—but do they really? Whether you and your man are totally different, or practically the same person, the bottom line is that you have to be able to come together on important decisions that impact your whole family. Test your partner and see how compatible you are as a team.

1 All the Advice

New couples get almost as much unsolicited advice as new parents. Your guy should be able to discern between the advice that's nonsense—but full of good intentions, of course—and the actual nuggets of help. Award him 1 point for correctly identifying which pieces of relationship advice are good, and which are garbage (answers in bold).

a) Good/Garbage: Never go to bed mad.

b) Good/**Garbage**: Tell each other everything. Everything.

c) Good/Garbage: Find ways to laugh together!

d) Good/**Garbage**: Just ignore your partner, and his or her bad behavior.

e) Good/Garbage: Make time for each other.

f) Good/**Garbage**: Always put your partner's feelings and needs first, and your own second.

Total Score _____ (0–6 pts)

2 Common Ground

Common ground gives you lots of fodder for great conversation, and lots of ways to connect. How much do you and your man have in common? Give him 1 point for each area of life in which you would say you are similar.

Level of education. ☐

Television preferences. ☐

Movie taste. ☐

Love of reading. ☐

Favorite cuisine. ☐

Pet picks. ☐

Drinking habits. ☐

Social lives. ☐

Working hours. ☐

Fashion favorites. ☐

Total Score ____ (0–10 pts)

3 Pet Peeves

No matter how much you have in common, or how close you are, there will always be those little things that get under each other's skin. Clipping fingernails, washing dishes using the wrong sponge, putting those tiny little stickers from fruit on the countertop … these are just a few of the things that can drive an otherwise loving couple completely insane. Choose the answer that best describes how your partner handles his pet peeves when you start to push his buttons.

He has so many pet peeves that you have no idea what you're doing to drive him crazy at any given moment.

NIL POINTS

He lets you know that you are annoying him by launching into his own set of annoying behaviors. **1 POINT**

He lets you know, loud and clear, that you are driving him bananas. **2 POINTS**

He just gets up and leaves for a few minutes if you are doing something that annoys him. **3 POINTS**

He tells you how much he loves you, and then tells you how much he hates what you are doing. **4 POINTS**

Total Score ____ (0–4 pts)

4 Activity: Man-Made Map

One of the number one fights that couples have is over navigation. Even with a smartphone feeding directions, some partners just cannot get along while taking even the simplest of outings together.

Ask your man to clearly map out directions to a destination of your choice, and see if he has what it takes to navigate. Award him up to 2 points for accuracy, details, and efficiency of route.

Map

Accuracy (0–2 pts)
Details (0–2 pts)
Efficiency of route (0–2 pts)
Total Score (0–6 pts)

CHAPTER EIGHT: SCORING

Add up your score on each question to get your total score for Chapter Eight, then find out how your man measures up below.

Q1 Score _____ (0–6 pts)

Q2 Score _____ (0–10 pts)

Q3 Score _____ (0–4 pts)

Q4 Score _____ (0–6 pts)

Total Chapter Score _____ (0–26 pts)

20–26 pts: Your compatibility score is off the charts! You and your man have so much in common, you're practically the same person. Freaky.

13–19 pts: You and your guy are very compatible in the most important areas. If you can find common ground and continue to appreciate one another's interests, you will never run out of things to talk about.

6–12 pts: Sometimes you're "on" and sometimes you're "off." To keep your relationship strong, keep the lines of communication open and make sure to listen to your man—and remind him to listen to you.

0–5 pts: Opposites attract, so they say, and you and your partner don't share too much in common. You may struggle sometimes to see eye-to-eye, but if you can be patient with one another, you'll learn a lot.

Chapter Nine

Crystal Ball

What will the future bring? You and your man may be on a long journey together, and wherever life takes you—there you'll be. Together! The ability to make plans and set goals that are achievable, exciting, and fun will keep you both fueled and committed. Test your man and see if you are in sync when it comes to looking into the future.

1 The Bucket List

In your twenties and thirties, it might feel as though life will go on forever—but eventually you'll find yourself at the end of life's road. Will you have completed all the things on your bucket list?

Step 1) Place a checkmark in the box on the left of each item below if it's something you want to add to your bucket list. You might want to substitute the suggestions below with your own dreams.

Step 2) Read the list to him and award him 1 point for each item that's on your bucket list that's also on his.

	You	Him
Fly a plane.	☐	☐
Travel to as many foreign countries as possible.	☐	☐
Cook an epic six-course meal.	☐	☐
Write a book, paint a painting, or create a sculpture.	☐	☐

	You	Him
Run a marathon/take part in a triathalon.	☐	☐
Scuba dive.	☐	☐
Explore the rainforest.	☐	☐
Learn to dance/learn martial arts.	☐	☐
Win a chess tournament.	☐	☐
Mentor someone.	☐	☐
Sing to an audience.	☐	☐
See the Northern Lights.	☐	☐
Go on a long road trip.	☐	☐
Own and decorate/furnish your own home.	☐	☐

**Total Number of Things
on Both Your Bucket Lists** _____ (0–14 pts)

2 Long-Term Plans

Your future is created by a thousand tiny decisions you take in the present moment. Every cent saved could go to a down payment on a house, and every night spent working instead of playing could add up to major career advances.

How does your man approach long-term plans? Choose the option below that sounds most applicable.

How can he think of the future when he's so hung up on everything that went wrong in the past? **NIL POINTS**

At breakfast, he plans as far as lunch. At lunch, he plans his afternoon snack. And so on. **1 POINT**

He likes to just see where life takes him rather than make plans. **2 POINTS**

He's got some vague, if unrealistic, ideas of what he'd like to be doing in ten years. **3 POINTS**

He has specific goals and measures his progress toward them regularly. **4 POINTS**

Total Score _____ (0–4 pts)

3 Cautiously Optimistic

Optimists see the glass as half-full. They are also more successful, healthier, and more resilient. On the other side, their Pollyanna attitude can be very annoying and exhausting for those who veer more toward the realistic side.

Is your partner an optimist or a pessimist? Award him
1 point each time he agrees with a statement below.

☐ When something goes right at work, your man attributes
it to his own hard work, not good luck.

☐ When something breaks around the house, your man
rarely gets mad at you or himself; he knows that things don't
last forever.

☐ Your man gets excited about little things, like a beautiful
sunset or a movie he likes on TV.

☐ Your man doesn't concentrate on the annoying little
things your family does; he's way more focused on spending
fun time together.

☐ If your man gets a call from an unknown number, he
answers it and chats in a friendly way with whomever is on
the other end, even if it's a salesperson.

Total Score _____ (0–5 pts)

4 Activity: Be Careful What You Wish For

A crystal ball, a winning lottery ticket, a magic bean—we all want a little something mystical and magical to help us along our path. If your guy found a magic lamp, rubbed it, and a genie offered him three wishes, ask him what he would wish for. Grade his answer from 0–2 for its altruism, creativity, and its appeal to you!

	ALTRUISM (0–2 PTS)	CREATIVITY (0–2 PTS)	APPEAL TO YOU (0–2 PTS)
Wish 1			
Wish 2			
Wish 3			
Total Score (0–18 pts)			

CHAPTER NINE: SCORING

Add up your score on each question to get your total score for Chapter Nine, then find out how your man measures up below.

Q1 Score _____ (0–14 pts)

Q2 Score _____ (0–4 pts)

Q3 Score _____ (0–5 pts)

Q4 Score _____ (0–18 pts)

Total Chapter Score _____ (0–41 pts)

31–41 pts: The future's so bright, you've gotta wear shades! You are in it for the long haul. You and your man can't wait to see what tomorrow brings, and you know that you'll be enjoying the journey together.

21–30 pts: Anything can happen, and your man is looking forward to finding out what's in store with you. Buckle up and enjoy the ride!

11–20 pts: Enjoy the here and now with your partner, and if you want to set goals, see the world, or try new things, just make it happen! For now, you and your guy are taking each day as it comes. Chances are that your man will follow you wherever you lead.

0–10 pts: Planning for the future isn't really your partner's claim to fame—if he's living in the moment, that's a good thing.

Chapter Ten

Sugar Daddy

Is your partner daddy material? Whether or not you already have rugrats, the questions in this chapter will help you evaluate your man's ability to successfully rear children. From choosing your child's name to keeping baby safe, can you come together on the most stressful (and sometimes rewarding) part of a relationship?

1 Taking Candy From a Baby

Baby proofing is half about keeping baby safe, and half about keeping mommy sane. According to current standards of baby safety, ask your man how he could keep baby safe.

Baby proofing is for suckers. Darwin will weed out the weak, so bring on the lighters, power tools, and cleaning chemicals.

NIL POINTS

Two words: Duct tape. **I POINT**

As long as baby stays in a playpen in the corner, there's really no need to babyproof the rest of the house. **2 POINTS**

He keeps the beer and lit candles out of reach, removes coins from the baby's mouth, and makes sure the power outlets remain fork-free. **3 POINTS**

He's a baby proofing wizard, from pool noodles on table legs to rubber bands or latches on kitchen cabinets. Nothing will stop him from creating a perfectly safe space for a little one.

4 POINTS

Total Score _____ (0–4 pts)

2 Diaper Duty

Who should be in charge of various household duties, from diapering to ballet practice? Talk it through with your man. For each of the duties that he's willing to take on, award him 1 point.

Dirty diaper duty. ☐

Meal time (especially cleaning up smashed peas!). ☐

Bath time. ☐

Bedtime stories. ☐

Middle of the night cuddles. ☐

Sick nurse. ☐

Little League coach. ☐

Ballet or dance instructor. ☐

Hair braider. ☐

School helper. ☐

Total Score ____ (0–10 pts)

3 Name That Babe

A name is probably the most important thing you give your child. Does your man know an Apple from a Penelope? Match the quirky baby names in the left-hand column with their meaning on the right—and while you're at it, maybe you'll get some ideas for naming your future babes! Award 1 point for each correct answer.

1. Portia		**a.** The red-haired warrior's son
2. Booth		**b.** Pig, hog, or doorway
3. Clancy		**c.** Dark one
4. Darcy		**d.** Lives in a hut

Total Score _____ (0–4 pts)

4 Activity: Speed Trials

Fatherhood can be intense. Time and rate your man from
0–2 points on the following activities. If you and/or your
partner already have kids, these activities can help hone
his skills.

Round 1) Use a kitchen towel or paper napkin to quickly
diaper a nearby object.

Precision _____ (0–2 pts)

Speed _____ (0–2 pts)

Flair _____ (0–2 pts)   **Total** _____ (0–6 pts)

Round 2) Set his alarm for 2A.M. and have him complete a
few simple tasks before you turn off the alarm.

Precision (0–2 pts)

Speed (0–2 pts)

Flair (0–2 pts)   **Total** _____ (0–6 pts)

Round 3) Use a belt to hold one of his hands behind his back. Have him prepare a meal and send a few emails.

Precision (0–2 pts)

Speed (0–2 pts)

Flair (0–2 pts)   **Total** _____ (0–6 pts)

Round 4) Watch a full episode of a child's television show and give a recap of the plot, characters, and values—is it suitable for your children?

Precision (0–2 pts)

Speed (0–2 pts)

Flair (0–2 pts)   **Total** _____ (0–6 pts)

                        Grand Total _____ (0–24 pts)

CHAPTER TEN: SCORING

Add up your score on each question to get your total score for Chapter Ten, then find out how your man measures up below.

Q1 Score _____ (0–4 pts)

Q2 Score _____ (0–10 pts)

Q3 Score _____ (0–4 pts)

Q4 Score _____ (0–24 pts)

Total Chapter Score _____ (0–42 pts)

30–42 pts: Oh, daddy! This guy is a true family man who loves the patter of tiny feet. Your man may be a contender for Father of the Year!

20–29 pts: He's got the raw talent and skills, now he just needs some practice. Your guy won't shy from changing diapers and is ready for all that family life can bring.

10–19 pts: The good news about parenting is that it's a learned art. What he lacks in skill, he makes up for in potential and promise. The main thing is he is willing to learn.

0–9 pts: It's possible your man was raised by wolves. You may need to work with him to teach him to love before you decide to reproduce. If you've already reproduced—just be patient with him, and know that it's OK to howl at the moon together sometimes!

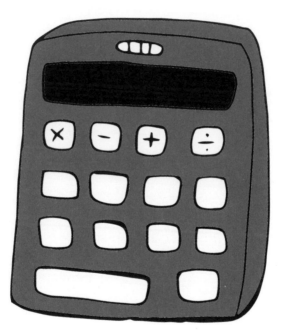

Total Score

Add up all your scores over the ten chapters and read the final results below.

	SCORE
Chapter One (0–46 pts)	
Chapter Two (0–32 pts)	
Chapter Three (0–42 pts)	
Chapter Four (0–36 pts)	
Chapter Five (0–39 pts)	
Chapter Six (0–25 pts)	
Chapter Seven (0–45 pts)	
Chapter Eight (0–26 pts)	
Chapter Nine (0–41 pts)	
Chapter Ten (0–42 pts)	
Total Score (0–374 pts)	

If he scored VERY HIGH
264–374 pts

Once in a while, a celebrity tabloid will publish a picture of a famous actor with his wife and family, and the entire population of women will see it and sigh and think, why can't my partner be like that? Stylish, devoted, adventurous, talented …

Well, that is precisely the feeling that you and your man give to all your friends and family. Enjoy it, but try not to rub it in anyone's face.

If he scored HIGH
175–263 pts

Your man's score says, I try to make her happy, but I'm still my own person. He hits all the vital notes to be a wonderful life partner, best friend, and lover. Whether you're cooking together, traveling, starting a family, or helping around the house—you and your man are in sync and full of love and respect for one another.

If he scored MEDIUM
86–174 pts

Your other half doesn't easily fit in a mold, and he's probably not overly concerned with what other people think about

him. He doesn't dote on you like a princess or a helpless child—which is a good thing. He views you as a partner! While you and your man may butt heads over little things, don't sweat the small stuff. It's not worth it to let little things come between you. Embrace your diamond in the rough and enjoy him for who he is—not who he isn't!

If he scored LOW
0–85 pts
One of the leading reasons relationships fail, according to one expert, is that people expect too much of one another. They expect the person to be a passionate lover, a perfect business partner, a best friend to whom they can tell all their secrets, a travel companion, a co-parent who is totally in sync, etc. You didn't choose your partner for his manners, his cooking skills, his romance, or his long-term planning. YOU know why you were attracted to him, and it's time to remember that reason. Was it his sense of humor, his bedroom moves, his intelligence? If there are things that trouble you in your relationship, you can work together to improve them over time. Your partner is just one man: It's possible he simply can't play all the roles in your life that you expect him to. If you need more friendship, find friends! If you need a workout buddy, find one! Then come home and focus on that special reason that you chose your man …